双双中文教材（12）
Chinese Language and Culture Course

中国古代故事 Ancient Chinese Stories

王双双 编著

王宜珈 画

北京大学出版社
PEKING UNIVERSITY PRESS

图书在版编目（CIP）数据

中国古代故事/王双双编著. —北京：北京大学出版社，2011.6
（双双中文教材12）
ISBN 978-7-301-08712-1

Ⅰ.中…　Ⅱ.王…　Ⅲ.汉语-对外汉语教学-教材　Ⅳ.H195.4

中国版本图书馆CIP数据核字（2005）第075447号

书　　　　名：	中国古代故事
著 作 责 任 者：	王双双　编著
英 文 翻 译：	王亦兵
责 任 编 辑：	邓晓霞
标 准 书 号：	ISBN 978-7-301-08712-1/H·1448
出 版 发 行：	北京大学出版社
地　　　　址：	北京市海淀区成府路205号　100871
网　　　　址：	http://www.pup.cn
电　　　　话：	邮购部 62752015　发行部 62750672　编辑部 62752028　出版部 62754962
电 子 信 箱：	zpup@pup.pku.edu.cn
印　刷　者：	北京大学印刷厂
经　销　者：	新华书店
	889毫米×1194毫米　16开本　8印张　140千字
	2006年9月第1版　2017年11月第5次印刷
定　　　　价：	76.00元（含课本、练习册和一张CD-ROM）

未经许可，不得以任何方式复制或抄袭本书之部分或全部内容。
版权所有，侵权必究
举报电话：（010）62752024
电子信箱：fd@pup.pku.edu.cn

前言

《双双中文教材》是一套专门为海外青少年编写的中文课本，是我在美国八年的中文教学实践基础上编写成的。在介绍这套教材之前，请读一首小诗：

> 一双神奇的手，
> 推开一扇窗。
> 一条神奇的路，
> 通向灿烂的中华文化。
>
> 鲍凯文 鲍维江
> 1998年

鲍维江和鲍凯文姐弟俩是美国生美国长的孩子，也是我的学生。1998年冬，他们送给我的新年贺卡上的小诗，深深地打动了我的心。我把这首诗看成我文化教学的"回声"。我要传达给海外每位中文老师：我教给他们（学生）中国文化，他们思考了、接受了、回应了。这条路走通了！

语言是交际的工具，更是一种文化和一种生活方式，所以学习中文也就离不开中华文化的学习。汉字是一种古老的象形文字，她从远古走来，带有大量的文化信息，但学起来并不容易。使学生增强兴趣、减小难度，走出苦学汉字的怪圈，走进领悟中华文化的花园，是我编写这套教材的初衷。

学生不论大小，天生都有求知的欲望，都有欣赏文化美的追求。中华文化本身是魅力十足的。把这宏大而玄妙的文化，深入浅出地，有声有色地介绍出来，让这迷人的文化如涓涓细流，一点一滴地渗入学生们的心田，使学生们逐步体味中国文化，是我编写这套教材的目的。

为此我将汉字的学习放入文化介绍的流程之中同步进行，让同学们在学中国地理的同时，学习汉字；在学中国历史的同时，学习汉字；在学中国哲学的同时，学习汉字；在学中国科普文选的同时，学习汉字……

这样的一种中文学习，知识性强，趣味性强；老师易教，学生易学。当学生们合上书本时，他们的眼前是中国的大好河山，是中国五千年的历史和妙不可言的哲学思维，是奔腾的现代中国……

总之，他们了解了中华文化，就会探索这片土地，热爱这片土地，就会与中国结下情缘。

最后我要衷心地感谢所有热情支持和帮助我编写教材的老师、家长、学生、朋友和家人，特别是老同学唐玲教授、何茜老师、我姐姐王欣欣编审及我女儿Uta Guo年复一年的鼎力相助。可以说这套教材是大家努力的结果。

王双双
2005年5月8日

说明

《双双中文教材》是一套专门为海外学生编写的中文教材。它是由美国加州王双双老师和中国专家学者共同努力，在海外多年的实践中编写出来的。全书共20册，识字量2500个，包括了从识字、拼音、句型、短文的学习，到初步的较系统的中国文化的学习。教材大体介绍了中国地理、历史、哲学等方面的丰富内容，突出了中国文化的魅力。课本知识面广，趣味性强，深入浅出，易教易学。全套书均有CD-ROM。

这套教材体系完整、构架灵活、使用面广。学生可以从零起点开始，一直学完全部课程20册；也可以将后11册（10～20册）的九个文化专题和第五册（汉语拼音）单独使用，这样便于高中和大学开设中国哲学、地理、历史等专门课程以及假期班、短期中国文化班、拼音速成班使用。

本教材符合了美国AP中文课程的目标和基本要求。

这本《中国古代故事》是《双双中文教材》的第十二册，课本适用于已学习掌握800多个汉字的学生。全书共九课，教程为12～16学时（每学时1.5～2小时）。

本书介绍了15个中国古代故事。故事情节曲折，带有传奇色彩，反映了古代中国人的生活习俗和风貌，以及他们的聪慧和幽默。学生们通过学习，进一步提高了中文水平，也感受到古代先贤的心胸和智慧，开阔了思维，得到了文化的传承。

本书介绍了常用连词、形容词的重叠，以及汉语中最常用的几种标点符号，同时又增加了组字练习。两段趣味汉字短文介绍了汉字由来及演变。

编者

课程设置

一年级	中文课本(第一册)	中文课本(第二册)	中文课本(第三册)
二年级	中文课本(第四册)	中文课本(第五册)	中文课本(第六册)
三年级	中文课本(第七册)	中文课本(第八册)	中文课本(第九册)
四年级	中国成语故事	中国地理常识	
五年级	中国古代故事	中国神话传说	
六年级	中国古代科学技术	中国文学欣赏	
七年级	中国诗歌欣赏	中文科普阅读	
八年级	中国古代哲学	中国历史(上)	
九年级	中国历史(下)	小说阅读，中文SAT II	
十年级	中文SAT II (强化班)	小说阅读，中文SAT II 考试	

目录

第一课　曹冲称象……………………………… 1

第二课　田忌赛马……………………………… 7

第三课　李寄杀蛇……………………………… 14

第四课　晏子使楚……………………………… 20

第五课　西门豹的故事………………………… 27

第六课　张良拾鞋……………………………… 35

第七课　三试华佗……………………………… 44

第八课　谁偷了茄子…………………………… 52

第九课　七步诗………………………………… 59

生字表　　……………………………………… 65

生词表　　……………………………………… 67

第一课

曹冲称象

古时候,有个人叫曹操,他是东汉末年①的政治家、军事家和诗人。有一次,人家送他一头大象。曹操非常高兴,带着儿子和官员们一同去看大象。

大象又高又大,身体像一面墙,腿像四根大粗柱子。这象到底有多重呢?官员们议论着。曹操问官员们:"谁能有办法把这头大象称一称?"

官员们有人说:"用一棵大树造一杆大秤来称,或者把大象宰了,切成一块一块的再称。"也有人说:"有了大秤也不成啊,谁有那么大的力气,提得起这杆大秤呢?再说,把大象宰了,虽然能称出它的重量,可是以后就再也没有大象了!"

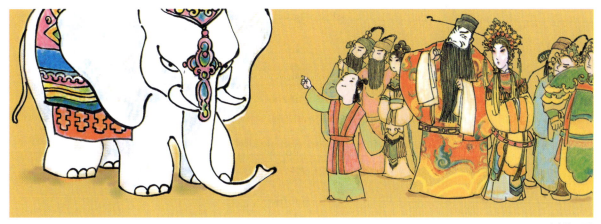

刘艺 画

① 东汉——也称后汉。中国历史上的一个朝代(公元25-220年)。

曹操听了官员们的话直摇头，说："难道就没有别的办法了吗？"曹操的儿子曹冲才六岁，他站出来说："我有好办法。"曹操连忙问儿子有什么办法。曹冲说："把大象赶到一艘大船上，看船身下沉了多少，就沿着水面在船舷上画一条线。再把大象赶上岸，往船上装石头，等船下沉到画线的地方，称一称船上的石头，就知道大象有多重了。"

曹操很高兴，说："这是个好办法。"于是叫人照着曹冲说的办法去做，果然称出了大象的重量。官员们一个个脸都红了，你看看我，我看看你，觉得自己还不如一个六岁的孩子。

生词

chōng 冲	firstname; rush	qiē 切	cut
chēng 称	weigh	nándào 难道	used in a rhetorical question for emphasis
guānyuán 官员	officer	liánmáng 连忙	promptly
dàodǐ 到底	on earth	gǎn 赶	drive
yìlùn 议论	discuss	sōu 艘	measure word for ships
gǎn 杆	measure word for balances, etc.	yánzhe 沿着	along
chèng 秤	balance	chuánxián 船舷	ship board
huòzhě 或者	or	guǒrán 果然	as expected
zǎi 宰	slay		

2

第一课

听写

曹冲　称　官员　沿着　果然　议论　切　或者　秤杆　*船弦　艘

注：*号以后的为听写选做题。

比一比

主 { 主人 / 主要 }　　柱 { 柱子 / 圆柱 }　　{ 称（称一称）/ 秤（一杆秤）}

称 { 称呼 / 称为 / 称一称 }　　员 { 官员 / 员工 / 飞行员 }

同音字

带　代　袋　戴

带 { 带着 / 带走 / 安全带 }　　代 { 代表 / 古代 / 第二代 }

袋 { 口袋 / 袋鼠 }　　　　戴 { 戴帽子 / 戴手表 }

字词运用

难道

难道你不知道老鼠怕猫吗？

你难道不知道明天有大风雪吗？

他能学会，难道我就学不会吗？

果然

昨天我就觉得可能要下雨，今天果然下雨了。

弟弟不听妈妈的话，不洗手就吃东西，果然生病了。

词语解释

果然——表示(shì)和事先想的一样。

议论——大家都说出各自的意见。

不如——比不上。

阅读

聪明的小曹冲

曹冲是曹操的一个儿子。一天，给曹操管马鞍(ān)的人发现马鞍被老鼠咬破了，他怕曹操生气，急得哭了。曹冲那时候才十岁，听说这件事以后，就对那人说："你别怕，后天中午，你去见我爸爸，我有办法救你。"

那人半信半疑，但是又没有别的办法，只好答应了。

曹冲回到家里，用小刀在自己的衣服上挖了几个小洞。看上去跟老鼠咬的一样。到了那天中午，曹冲穿上了这件衣服，装作很不高兴的样子，走到曹操跟前。曹操问他："冲儿，你怎么不高兴啊？"曹冲指着衣服，说："你看，衣服叫老鼠咬破了。别人都说，穿老鼠咬破的衣服，人要生大病。"

曹操笑着说，"冲儿，那是骗人的，别相信它。"正说着，管马鞍的人进来了，说马鞍给老鼠咬了。要是平常，曹操就要生气了。可是这一回，他不但没生气，反而笑起来，说："老鼠嘛(ma)，还管得住它咬东西？你看我儿子的衣服，天天穿在身上，都被老鼠咬破了，更不用说马鞍子了。"

Lesson One   Cao Chong Weighing the Elephants

In ancient China, there was a man named Cao Cao, a politician, strategist and poet in the period of the Eastern Han Dynasty. One day, an elephant was sent to him as a gift and he felt so happy that he went to see the elephant with his sons and officers together.

The elephant was very tall and heavy, with body like a wall and four legs like thick logs. Seeing this, officers began to wonder what weight this big elephant would be. Then Cao Cao asked, "Who can think out a way to weigh the elephant?"

Some officers answered, "We can cut down a big tree to make a scale, or we can kill the elephant and cut it into pieces, then we can weigh it. " Others questioned, "Even we have such a big scale, who can be strong enough to carry it? Moreover, if killing it, we can know the weight, but we will lose it forever!"

Hearing all of this, Cao Cao shook his head and continued to ask, "Isn't there any other way?" His son, Cao Chong, who is only six years old, came out to say, "I have a good idea." Cao Cao hurried to ask what it is. Cao Chong said, "First, drive the elephant to a ship and mark where the ship has sunk. Then, drive back the elephant and put some stones into the ship. When the ship sank where it is marked, then we can just weigh how much the stones weigh, we can get to figure out the weight of the elephant. "

"That's a good idea," exclaimed Cao Cao. Then he ordered the others to do as what Cao Chong said. Finally, they got the weight of the elephant. All the officers turned flushed, looking at each other and feeling that they are not as intelligent as a six-year-old child.

Clever Little Cao Chong

One day, the man who took care of Cao Cao's saddle found that rats gnawed some holes in the saddle and was worried to cry because he was afraid Cao Cao would get angry about it. This issue was made known to Cao Chong, one of Cao Cao's sons, who was only 10 years old at that time. After hearing it, he comforted that man, saying "Don't worry. You may visit my father at noon the day after tomorrow. I can help you."

Although the man was not quite convinced, he had no choice but to accept the suggestion.

When Cao Chong came home, he cut some holes in his own clothes by knife and made them look like the holes gnawed by rats. By that noon, wearing this clothes, Cao Chong went to visit his father and pretended to be unhappy. Cao Cao asked, "Dear, what's the matter with you?" Pointing at the clothes, Cao Chong answered, "Look, rats gnawed my clothes. It is said that people will get sick if their clothes are gnawed by rats ".

Cao Cao said with a laugh, "Dear Chong, that's not true. Don't believe it." Just at this time, the man taking care of saddles came up, telling Cao Cao that the saddle was gnawed by rats. Hearing this, Cao Cao, who would be very angry if on other occasions, just broke into laughter, saying "The rats, who can be in charge of them? Look, my son's clothes, is also gnawed by rats although he wears it every day, let alone the saddles."

第二课

田忌赛马

齐国的大将田忌喜欢赛马。有一回他和齐威王比赛。他们把各自的马分成上、中、下三等。比赛的时候，田忌用自己的上等马对齐王的上等马，用中等马对齐王的中等马，用下等马对齐王的下等马。由于齐威王每个等级的马都比田忌的强，三场比赛下来，田忌都输了。他垂头丧气，正要离开赛马场，田忌的好朋友孙膑(bìn)走过来说："从刚才的比赛看，大王的马比你的快不了多少呀……你再同他赛一次，我有办法让你赢。"田忌问孙膑："你是说再换几匹马？"孙膑胸有成竹地说："一匹也不用换。你就照

薛智广 画

我的主意办吧。"

齐威王正在得意洋洋地夸自己的马，看见田忌和孙膑走过来，便说："怎么，难道你失败了还不服气？"田忌说："当然不服气，咱们再赛一次！"齐威王说："那就来吧！"

一声锣响，赛马又开始了。孙膑让田忌先用下等马对齐威王的上等马，第一场输了。第二场，孙膑让田忌拿上等马对齐威王的中等马，赢了第二场。第三场田忌拿中等马对齐威王的下等马，又赢了一场。这下，田忌赢两场输一场，赢了齐威王。还是原来的马，只调换了一下出场顺序，就可转败为胜。

生词

jì 忌	first name; envy		luó 锣	gong
dà jiàng 大将	general		dì yī chǎng 第一场	the first round
gè zì 各自	each		yíng 赢	win
děng jí 等级	grade		diào huàn 调换	exchange
shū 输	lose		shùn xù 顺序	order
chuí tóu sàng qì 垂头丧气	be dejected		zhuǎn bài wéi shèng 转败为胜	turn loss into gain
shī bài 失败	be defeated			

听写

垂头丧气　失败　输　顺序　转败为胜　各自　调换　等级　*赢

比一比

齐 { 齐全 / 整齐 }　　开 { 开始 / 离开 }　　胜 { 胜利 / 名胜古迹 }

赛 { 比赛 / 赛马 / 篮球赛 }　　顺 { 顺利 / 顺序 / 顺路 }　　换 { 交换 / 调换 / 换衣服 }

反义词

强——弱　　失败——成功　　输——赢

胜——败　　垂头丧气——得意洋洋

多音字

将 jiāng { 将军 / 将来 }　　将 jiàng { 大将 / 少将 }

词语解释

垂头丧气——低着头，没有精神，很不高兴。

转败为胜——眼看要失败的事情，经过努力变为胜利。

阅读

有趣的汉字（一）

汉字为什么是这个样子？汉字看起来怎么像一个个小图画？不错，汉字不是拼音文字，而是从象形文字发展而来的。那么，什么是象形文字呢？如果你学过画画，用画家的眼光去看汉字，你会发现，许多汉字如"口"、"爪"、"田"……，真的很像真实的东西。

远古的时候，生活在中国这片土地上的人们，是用简单的图画来记录生活的。比如"日"这个字，最早是一幅画。"月"这个字，最早它也是一幅画。这些图画是汉字的源头。想知道汉字的起源，还要从甲骨文和金文说起。

甲骨文

什么是甲骨文？甲骨文是3 000多年前在中国使用的一种古文字。那时没有纸，这些字被人用刀刻在龟壳上或牛骨上，所以称为甲骨文。现在，人们从这些龟甲和牛骨上发现的单字有5 000多个，其中3 000多个已被文字学家认出。

金文

金文也叫钟鼎(dǐng)文,是3 000多年前中国人铸(zhù)在或刻在青铜器上的文字。早期的金文和甲骨文很相近。

请看下图,这样可以清楚地了解汉字是怎样被创(chuàng)造并发展的。

汉字演变

象形文字	甲骨文	小篆	隶书	简体
☼	日	⊙	日	日
☽	月	月	月	月
⛰	山	山	山	山
≋	水	水	水	水
羊	羊	羊	羊	羊
馬	馬	馬	馬	马
車	車	車	車	车
子	子	子	子	子

Lesson Two Tian Ji Racing Horse with the King

Tian Ji, the general of Qi State, likes horseracing. One day, he had a race with the King Qi Wei Wang. They rated their horses into three categories: the upper class, the middle class and the lower class. In the race, Tian Ji's upper class horses will race with the King's upper class horses, the middles with the middles and the lower class with the lower class. Due to the fact that the King's horses at each level are all stronger than Tian Ji's, Tian Ji could not win the race in three matches. When Tian Ji was going to leave the racing ground with head dropped down, his good friend Sun Bin came over and comforted him, "Just now I can see the King's horses do not run much faster than yours! Just race with him again and I can help you win." "Do you mean changing some better horses?" Tian Ji asked. "No, you needn't change even one horse. Just do as I say." said Sun Bin, with a well-thought-out plan in mind.

Then they went together to see the King, who was immensely proud of his own horses. Seeing them, the King asked, "What's the matter? Aren't you convinced yet? " Tian Ji said, "Surely not. Can we have a race again?" "All right, " answered the King.

The horse racing began with one sound of gong. In the first round, Sun Bin used Tian Ji's lower class horses to compete with the King's upper class horses and Tian Ji lost it as expected. In the second round, Sun Bin used Tian Ji's upper class horses to compete with the King's middle class horses and Tian Ji won it. In the third round, Tian Ji used his middle class horses to compete with the King's lower class horses and again beat the King's horses. As a result, Tian Ji won twice and lost once, winning over the King. It reveals that failure can be turned into success when just changing the order of competing, even with the same horses.

Interesting Chinese Characters (1)

People may wonder why Chinese characters look like some small pictures. In fact, Chinese characters originate from pictographs instead of phonetic language. What is pictograph? If you know something about painting and study the characters from an artist's perspective, you may find some characters like "口"、"爪"、"田" look much like real objects.

In ancient times, those ancient Chinese usually drew some simple pictures to keep a record of events. For example, Chinese characters "日" referring to sun and "月"referring to moon were pictures originally. Therefore, pictures are considered to be the origin of Chinese characters, which can be traced back to the oracle-bone characters and bronzeware characters.

Oracle-bone characters

What is oracle-bone character? It is a kind of ancient Chinese character used in China about 3,000 years ago. At that time, when there was no paper, the characters were carved on the tortoise shells or bull's bones, so they were called oracle-bone characters. Up to now we have found more than 5,000 characters on the oracle bones, 3,000 of which have been recognized by philologist.

Bronzeware Characters

Bronzeware character, also called "Zhongding Wen", is a kind of ancient Chinese characters carved or cast on bronze objects. Bronzeware characters and oracle-bone characters in early times are very similar to each other.

Bronzeware characters and oracle-bone characters in the upper diagram can show us how the Chinese characters have been created and evolved.

中国古代故事

第三课

李寄杀蛇

汉朝时,南方一座山中有一条很大的毒蛇,经常出来伤人。官府派人杀蛇,不但没有杀死蛇,去的人反倒让毒蛇吃掉了几个,因此人们都十分害怕这条蛇。

后来巫婆说蛇要吃十二三岁的女孩,官府只好出钱买女孩,由巫婆送到蛇洞口。已经有12名女孩活活被蛇吃掉了。

薛智广 画

有个小女孩叫李寄,她只有十三岁,却胆大过人。她向父母提出来要去杀蛇除害。父母死活不同意。她自己跑到官府说她想杀蛇为民除害。官府见她是个少女,不同意她去,后来看她一定要去,就同意了。李寄说她要一把最好的宝剑和一条会咬蛇的猎狗,于是官府给了她一把青龙剑和一只凶猛的猎狗。

李寄回家,做了许多饭团,准备到时候用。那天清早,李寄让人把饭团搬到蛇洞口,自己一手握着剑,一手拉着狗等在洞口。其他人早就跑远了。

不一会儿,毒蛇出现了。这蛇有七八丈长,两只眼睛射出凶光。蛇闻到饭团的香味,张开大口吞吃。这时李寄放出猎狗,猎狗扑向毒蛇咬起来。李寄在毒蛇和猎狗咬斗的时候,一个箭步跳起,高举青龙剑向蛇背砍去。蛇回头要咬李寄,猎狗又扑上去咬住了大蛇。大蛇用力甩动身子,想把猎狗甩下来。李寄对准毒蛇的身子、尾巴连砍多剑。大蛇鲜血溅出,死在洞外。

聪明勇敢的李寄杀死了毒蛇,为民除了害。老百姓感谢她,把她的故事编成歌,一直传唱着。

中国古代故事

生词

jì 寄	first name, mail		dòu 斗	fight
shā 杀	kill		jǔ 举	hold up
dú 毒	poisonous		kǎn 砍	chop
guān fǔ 官府	local authorities		xiān xuè 鲜血	blood
wū pó 巫婆	witch		jiàn 溅	splash
dǎn dà 胆大	audacious		yǒnggǎn 勇敢	brave
chú hài 除害	rid of scourge		biān 编	compose
jiàn 剑	sword			
zhàng 丈	a unit of length (=3⅓ metres)			

听写

李寄　杀　毒蛇　除害　举剑　鲜血　勇敢　砍　斗　*编

比一比

毒 { 毒药 / 有毒 }　　　府 { 官府 / 政府 }　　　步 { 进步 / 箭步 }

传 { 传说 / 传唱   丈 { 丈夫 / 一丈   敢 { 不敢 / 勇敢

握 { 握手 / 握着   感 { 感谢 / 感动   { 交（交换）（交朋友） / 校（学校） / 咬（咬人） / 狡（狡猾）

进口歌

"才"字进口成一"团"，

"元"字进口逛花"园"，

"大"字进口找原"因"，

"冬"字进口画"图"画，

"玉"字进口建"国"家，

"员"字进口大团"圆"。

中国古代故事

阅读

有趣的汉字（二）

如果你来到中国南方的农村，可以看到这样的自然风景：方块的水田里长着水稻。中国人种水稻已有几千年了。"田"字的写法，不正像我们看到的稻田吗？

田字还可以组成许多字。比如"男"字，是由"田"和"力"组成的。这让人想到古代中国是个农业国家，大部分的男人是在田地里劳动，而把田地种好是要花力气的。

"子"字，在甲骨文中，就像一个婴(yīng)儿的形象。这古老的字形使母亲们想到自己孩子小时候的样子：大大的头和一个可爱的小身体。

"女"和"子"组成"好"字。想一想，一个女人有了孩子不是很幸福，很好的事吗？

薛智广 画

Lesson Three   Li Ji Killing the Poisonous Snake

In Han Dynasty, there was a huge poisonous snake in a mountain in the south which often came out to hurt people. So the local authorities sent some people to kill the snake, but it turned out that the snake was not killed while some of the would-be-snake-killers were eaten by the snake. As a result, people were scared by this snake.

Later on, a witch said the problem could be solved if some girls at 12 or 13 years old were sent to be eaten by the snake. Thus, the local authorities bought some girls and the witch sent them to the mouth of the cave for the snake to eat. Altogether there were 12 girls eaten alive by the snake.

Such tragedy deeply impressed a girl named Li Ji who is only 13 years old but very brave. She told her parents she would go to kill the snake, but her parents refused her request. Then she went to the local government and suggested she should kill the snake for the people. Seeing she is only a girl, the government doesn't accept her proposal, but her persistence makes the government agree to offer her one sharp sword and a savage hunting dog which can bite the snake as Li Ji's request.

Coming back home, Li Ji made some rice dumplings for preparation. Early in the morning, Li Ji had the rice dumplings moved to the month of the cave, waiting there with the sword in one hand and the hunting dog in another hand. All the rest people ran far away.

A moment later, the poisonous snake came up. It was about seven or eight zhang long(equal to 23 to 25 meters), having a fierce and ruthless look in two eyes. Attracted by the smell of rice dumplings, the snake began to eat with big bites, when Li Ji let go the hunting dog to fight with the snake. In the twinkling of an eye, Li Ji took up the sword and cut the back of snake with great effort. When the snake turned its head and tried to bite Li Ji, the hunting dog hurried to bite the snake. The snake shook its body, trying to get off the hunting dog. At this moment, Li Ji aimed at its body and tail and cut them with the sword many times, which made the snake blood and die finally at the outside of the cave.

The clever and brave Li Ji killed the poisonous snake, which moved the public. They made her story into a song which has been singing all the time to show their gratitude.

Interesting Chinese Characters (2)

When you come to the countryside in the south of China, you may view such sceneries: rice is growing in the square-shaped fields. It has been thousands of years since Chinese began to grow rice. Doesn't the Chinese character "田" look like the rice fields that come into our sight?

"田"can make many other characters, such as "男", which is made up of "田" (field) and "力" (strength). It reminds people that ancient China is an agriculture country, where most men had to work in the fields. It takes men great strength to grow good crops.

The character "子" looks like an image of a baby in oracle-bone character. The ancient inscriptions reminds mother of what the baby is like : a big head and a lovely little body.

Another character "好" is made up of "女" (woman; female) and "子" (child). Just imagine, isn't it happy and good for a woman to have a child?

中国古代故事

第四课

晏子使楚
（yàn）

春秋时期，齐国和楚国都是大国。有一回，齐王派大夫晏子出使到楚国去。楚王觉得自己是强国，想借机侮辱晏子，显示一下楚国的威风。

楚王知道晏子个子矮小，就叫人在城门旁边开了一个五尺高的小门。晏子来到楚国，楚王叫人关上城门，让晏子从这个小门进去。晏子看了看说："这是个狗洞，不是城门，只有访问'狗国'才从狗洞进去。"话传到楚王那里，楚王只好让人打开城门把晏子迎接进去。

薛智广 画

晏子进宫见了楚王，楚王冷冷地说："难道齐国没有人了吗？"晏子说："我国首都的人都把袖子举起来，就能连成一片云；大家都甩一把汗，就能下一阵雨；街上的行人一个跟着一个。大王怎么说齐国没有人呢？"楚王说："既然有这么多人，为什么让你来呢？"晏子说："我国有个规矩：访问上等的国家，就派上等人去；访问下等的国家，就派下等人。我最不中用，就派到这儿来了。"楚王听了只好苦笑。

一天，楚王和晏子一起喝酒。正喝得高兴时，见两个卫士带着一个犯人走过。楚王问："那人犯的什么罪？是哪里人？"卫士说："是强盗，齐国人。"楚王嘲笑地对晏子说："齐国人怎么能干这种事情？"楚国的大臣们也跟着笑了。晏子站起来说："大王可听说过，淮(huái)南的柑子，又大又甜。可是这种树一种到淮北，就只能结又小又苦的枳(zhǐ)①，这是因为水土不同。同样的道理，齐国人在齐国能安居乐业好好劳动，一到楚国，就做起强盗来了，也许是两国的水土不同吧。"楚王听了说："我原来想取笑大夫，没想到反让大夫取笑了。"

从这以后，楚王不敢不尊重晏子了。

---

① 枳——一种味道酸苦的果实。

中国古代故事

生词

chū shǐ 出使	be sent on a diplomatic mission	jì rán 既然	since
jiè jī 借机	take the opportunity	guī ju 规矩	rule
wǔ rǔ 侮辱	insult	fàn rén 犯人	prisoner, criminal
xiǎn shì 显示	display	fàn zuì 犯罪	commit a crime
wēi fēng 威风	power and prestige	qiáng dào 强盗	robber
ǎi xiǎo 矮小	short	gān zi 柑子	mandarin orange
fǎng wèn 访问	visit	ān jū lè yè 安居乐业	live and work in peace and contentment
yíng jiē 迎接	welcome	qǔ xiào 取笑	ridicule, make fun of
xiù zi 袖子	sleeve	zūn zhòng 尊重	respect

听写

出使　访问　迎接　袖子　既然　取笑　矮小　显示

安居乐业　*尊重　犯罪

比一比

楚 { 楚国 / 清楚　　　迎 { 迎接 / 欢迎　　　尊 { 尊重 / 尊敬

转 { 转动 / 转来转去   传 { 传话 / 传唱   专 { 专家 / 专业

句型

既然……就……

既然……也……

既然……还……

1. 你既然知道错了，就应当马上改正。
2. 既然你一定要去，我也不拦(lán)你了。
3. 你既然不喜欢这个电影，为什么还来看？

词语解释

侮辱——当面嘲笑对方，表示看不起、不尊重对方。

不中用——没有用。

犯人——犯罪的人。

嘲笑——用言语笑话别人。

安居乐业——安定地生活，愉快地工作。

包青天

北宋时，出了一位著名的清官，叫包拯，老百姓都叫他"包公"或"包青天"。

一天，有个叫刘全的农民跑来告状，说他家的一头耕牛，不知道叫谁给割掉了舌头，眼看活不成了，请求包公追查。

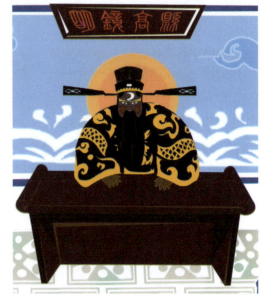

包公听刘全讲了事情的经过，就对刘全说："你把牛宰了卖肉吧！"刘全失望地走了。当时官府是不让杀耕牛的。因为是包公让宰的，刘全回家后就把牛杀了。

过了几天，有个人来向包公告状说："刘全把他家的耕牛杀了。"包公听了问他："你知道刘全为什么要杀耕牛吗？"那人说："不知道，不过听人家说是牛舌头被人割了。"包公一听，就明白了，沉下脸来说："是你割了他家的牛舌头，还不赶快认罪！"

告状人大吃一惊，看到事情已被发现，只得认罪。

原来包公听了刘全的话，知道是有人想要害他，于是，故意让刘全回去把牛杀了，好让这个人以为割牛舌头的事查不出来了，再借杀耕牛的事来害刘全。果然那个割牛舌头的人就来告状了，结果被包公抓到了。

 English Translation

Lesson Four Yan Zi Visting Chu State as an Ambassador

During the period of Spring and Autumn, Qi State and Chu State were both powerful states. Once the king of Qi State sent his senior official Yan Zi to visit Chu State, whose king felt that his country was powerful and decided to insult Yan Zi in order to display his country's power and prestige.

Knowing that Yan Zi was short, the king of Chu opened up a five-chi high cave beside the city gate and asked Yan Zi to go through this cave when Yan Zi arrived. After having a look at the cave, Yan Zi said, "This is a dog's cave and not the city gate. If I visit the dog's country, then I just go through this cave." Words spread to the ears of the king and he had to open the city gate to welcome Yan Zi.

When Yan Zi met the king of Chu, the king of Chu asked coldly, "Aren't there any other people in Qi State?" "Sure. In the capital of Qi State, if people just raise their sleeves, they can form a wide range of cloud; if they just wipe off their sweat, they can form a shower. There are crowds of people in the street. How can Your Majesty ask such a question?" said Yan Zi. "Since that is the case, why are you sent here?" The king of Chu continued to ask. Yan Zi answered, "There is a rule in our country: when visiting a superior country, a person of higher class will be sent; when visiting an inferior country, a person of lower class will be sent. Since I am the most useless, I was sent here." It made the king of Chu can do nothing but give a wry smile.

One day, the king of Chu had a dinner with Yan Zi. While they were enjoying the meal, two soldiers escorted a criminal to pass in front of them. The king of Chu asked, " What crime does he commit? Where is he form? " The soldiers answered, "He is a robber from Qi State." Hearing this, the king of Qi state asked Yan Zi with sneer, "How can people of Qi State do such a disgraceful thing?" With the words all the ministers laughed. At this moment, Yan Zi stood up, explaining calmly, "Has Your Majesty ever heard such a story? The orange, when growing in Huai Nan, is very big and sweet. But when such tree is planted in Huai Bei, it can only grow small and bitter fruit. The reason is that climate and natural environment make the difference. Such case can also be applied into our case. When people are living in Qi State, they are working very hard and living happily; but when they come to Chu State, they become the robbers, maybe because the different countries make so." Hearing this, the king of Chu said convincedly, "I am so sorry. I intended to deride you, but I didn't expect that I asked for a snub. "

From that time on, the king of Chu State dared not cold-shoulder Yan Zi any more.

Bao Qing Tian

In the Northern Song Dynasty, there was a famous honest and upright official named Bao Zheng, who was famous for being just-minded, so the public called him "Bao Gong" or "Bao Qing Tian (the just-minded magistrate)".

One day, a peasant named Liu Quan came to ask for help from Bao Gong, telling him that the tongue of his ox was cut off and the ox would die soon. He pleaded for close investigation of this case.

After hearing the details of the whole case, Bao Gong told Liu Quan to kill the ox and sell the beef, which made Liu Quan very disappointed. At that time, the ox for ploughing the field was not permitted to be killed, but Bao Gong told Liu Quan to do so, he just obeyed and killed the ox when going back home.

Several days later, a person came to sue Liu Quan for killing the ox. Then Bao Gong asked him, "Do you know why he killed the ox?" The man answered, "I don't know, but I hear that the tongue of his ox has been cut off". Hearing this word, Bao Gong understood everything, pulling a long face, questioning the person "It must be you who cut off the tongue. Why not hurry to admit your guilt?"

The man was greatly shocked and had to plead guilty since he found everything has come out in the open.

For this case, Bao Gong has made such an inference: Liu Quan's words revealed that somebody wanted to send him up. In order to find out who made it, Bao Gong deliberately told Liu Quan to kill the ox so that the man would think nobody knew who had cut off the ox's tongue and on the contrary, came to bring an action against Liu Quan for killing the ox. Just as expected, that man who had cut off the ox's tongue really came to sue Liu Quan and got caught at last by Bao Gong.

第五课

西门豹的故事

战国时期,魏国的国王派西门豹去管理一个地方。西门豹到了那里,看到土地荒了,人口很少,就找了位老人,问是怎么回事。老人说:"都是河神娶亲给闹的。漳(zhāng)河的神,每年要娶个年轻漂亮的姑娘。要是不给他送,漳河就要发大水,把田地全淹了。"

西门豹问:"这是谁说的?"老人说:"巫婆说的。官绅每年都给河神办喜事,硬让老百姓出钱。他们每次要收几百万钱,可是只花二三十万办喜事,多下来的钱就跟巫婆分了。"西门豹又

薛智广 画

问:"新娘是从哪儿来的?"老人说:"哪家有年轻的女孩儿,巫婆就带着人到哪家去挑选。有钱的人家花点钱就过去了,没钱的只好眼看着女孩儿被他们拉走。到了河神娶亲的那天,他们让打扮好的女孩儿坐在草席上,顺水漂去。开始,草席还是浮着的,到了河中心,草席连女孩儿就一起沉下去了。有女儿的人家都逃到外地去了。这里的人口越来越少,地方也越来越穷。"西门豹想了想说:"下一回河神娶亲,告诉我一声,我也去送送新娘。"

到了河神娶亲的日子,漳河边上站满了老百姓。西门豹真的带着卫士来了,巫婆和当地的官绅们急忙迎接。

西门豹说:"把新娘领来让我看看。"巫婆把新娘领过来,西门豹一看,女孩满脸泪水。他对巫婆说:"不行,这个姑娘不漂亮,河神不会满意的。请你去跟河神说一声,说我要另选个漂亮的,过几天送去。"说完,叫卫士抱起巫婆把她扔进了漳河。巫婆在河里扑腾(teng)了几下就沉下去了。等了一会儿,西门豹对官绅的头子说:"巫婆怎么还不回来?请你去催一催吧。"说完,又叫卫士把那个人也扔进了漳河。

西门豹面对着漳河站了很久。那些官绅都吓得连气也不敢出。西门豹回过头来看着他们说:"怎么还不回来?请你们去催

催吧。"说着又要叫卫士把他们扔进漳河去。这些官绅一个个吓得面如土色，跪下求饶。西门豹说："起来吧，看样子是河神把他们留下了。你们都回去吧。"老百姓明白了，巫婆和官绅都是骗钱害人的。

西门豹带领老百姓开了十二条水渠，引漳河的水浇田，每年的收成都很好。从那以后漳河再也没有发过大水。老百姓从此安居乐业。

生词

bào	豹	leopard	dǎ ban	打扮	dress up
wèi	魏	Wei State	cǎo xí	草席	straw mat
guǎn lǐ	管理	manage	lèi shuǐ	泪水	tear
huāng	荒	barren	cuī	催	hasten, urge
qǔ qīn	娶亲	take a wife	guì xià	跪下	fall on one's knee
yān	淹	flood, submerge	qiú ráo	求饶	beg for mercy
guān shēn	官绅	officer	shuǐ qú	水渠	ditch; aqueduct
yìng	硬	force	jiāo tián	浇田	irrigate the field
xīn niáng	新娘	bride			

中国古代故事

听写

管理　娶亲　淹了　硬　打扮　泪水　催　水渠　*草席

比一比

{ 取（取笑） / 娶（娶亲） }　{ 荒（荒地） / 慌（慌张） }　{ 浇（浇水） / 饶（求饶） }　{ 危（危险） / 跪（跪下） }

字词运用

遍　骗　编

这个电影我已经看过两遍了。

狐狸骗乌鸦说："你有五彩的羽毛，真漂亮！"

我过生日，姐姐编了一本小画书送给我，我可喜欢了。

反义词

硬——软　　本地——外地　　迎接——欢送

高——矮　　胆大——胆小　　喜事——丧事(sāng)

句型

不论……都……

小春不论画什么都很像。

小梅不论做什么都是又快又好。

不论你说什么他都不听。

要是……就……

明天要是刮风下雪，我们就不出去了。

要是你喜欢这件衣服，就买了吧。

昨天要是你开车，就不会出事了。

词语解释

发大水——下雨太多，江河湖中的水流出来。

官绅——官员和当地有钱、有名的人。

喜事——使人高兴的事，本文特指结婚(hūn)。

催——叫人快一点。

收成——稻子、麦子、棉花、蔬菜、水果等农作物的产量。

中国古代故事

阅读

快刀斩乱麻(zhǎn)

古时候有个人叫高欢。一天，他把几个儿子叫来，给他们每人一团乱麻说："我给你们每个人一团麻，看你们谁能把麻理整齐。"说完就坐在旁边，看他们怎么办。几个儿子拿着乱麻，有的急得满头大汗，有的干脆(cuì)把麻扔在一边，不理了。高欢看到这些，心想："这几个孩子，连一团乱麻都理不好，长大了还能干什么呢？"

薛智广　画

这时候，二儿子高洋说："请父亲给我一把剑。"高欢不知道儿子要剑做什么，就把腰上的宝剑给了他。高洋接过剑，把那团乱麻放在地上，一剑砍下去，乱麻被切成了两段。高欢问："你这是干什么？高洋说："要想把一团乱麻理清，完全是浪费时间。我把它从中间切断，您看，断的地方麻头不是整齐了吗？"

fèi

高欢连连点头说，"对呀！对呀！快刀斩乱麻，整齐清楚，是个解决难题的好办法啊！"

高洋长大以后，做了北齐的皇帝。

Lesson Five The Story of Ximen Bao

During the period of Warring States, the king of Wei State sent an officer named Ximen Bao to govern a place. When Ximen Bao arrived there, he saw few people living on the wasteland and therefore went to ask an old man for the truth. The old man said, "It is all caused by the so-called God of River, who will marry a young beautiful girl every year. Otherwise, God of Zhang He River will flood all the fields."

Then Ximen Bao asked, "Who said so?" "The witch. So the officers will hold wedding ceremony for the God of River every year and levy millions of money from the public. After spending 200,000-300,000 for the ceremony, the officers will split the rest of money with the witch. " "Where does the bride come from?" asked Ximen Bao. The old man answered, "The witch takes some followers to the families and grabs the girls. For wealthy families, they can pay some money and save the girls; but for poor families, the parents have no choice but to see them take the girls away. On the wedding day, they will dress the bride up and drift the girl away on the straw mat with the current. At first, the straw mat is floating and when it comes to the center of the river, it will sink down with the girl. So the families where there are girls have fled away to other places and few people stay here, becoming poorer and poorer. " Pondering over these words for a moment, Xi'men Bao said, "Next time when God of River has the wedding day, just let me know and I'll send my regards to the bride."

When it comes to the wedding day, the crowds stood beside the river. And Xi'men Bao really came with his followers, which made the witch and local officers hurry to welcome them.

Ximen Bao said, "Take the bride here and let me have a look." The witch led the girl, who is in tears, to the side of Ximen Bao. Ximen Bao said to the witch, "Oh, no. This girl is not beautiful enough to satisfy the God of River. Please go to tell the God of River that I'll choose another more beautiful girl for him and send her there a few days later." With the words, Ximen Bao asked the followers to throw the witch into the river, who immediately sank down after struggling for a few minutes. After a while, Ximen Bao said to the head of local officers, "Why hasn't the witch been back yet? Please go to urge her." Then the followers obeyed the order and threw that man into the river.

Facing the river, Ximen Bao stood there for a long time. All the officers were scared out of breath. Turning his head to look at them, Ximen Bao said, "Why are they not back? You go to hurry them." With the words, he was going to ask the followers to throw them into the river. All the officers were scared to death and begged for mercy on their knees. Then Ximen Bao said, "Stand up and go back. Maybe the God of River has asked them to stay there." Only until now do the public come to understand the witch and officers had cheated their money and done a great harm to them.

Ximen Bao guided people to hew out twelve ditches to lead the water into the filed, which made good harvests every year. After that, the river has never been flooded. People are living in peace and contentment.

Cut the Gordian Knot

In ancient times, there was a man named Gao Huan. One day, he called his sons and gave each of them a tangled skein of jute, said "I give each one of you a tangled skein of jute and see how you can sort it out." With the words, he sat beside and watched them how to do with it. Several sons took the tangled skein of jute, and tried to put it in order, but failed. Some of them were sweated, some of them just threw it away and gave up. Seeing this, Guan Huan thought by himself, "These sons, what can they do when growing up if they even can't sort out the tangled skein of jute?"

Just at this time, the second son Gao Yang turned his body and said to his father, "Please give me a sword." Not knowing why he needs the sword, Gao Huan just took off the sword from his own waist and gave it to Gao Yang. Taking the sword, Gao Yang put the tangled skein of jute on the ground and cut it into two halves by sword. "Why do you do like this?" asked Gao Huan. Gao Yang answered, "It is totally a waste of time to sort out the tangled skein of jutes. If I just cut it in the middle, look, isn't it orderly in the place where it is cut?"

Nodding his head repeatedly, Gao Huan said, "Yes, that's true. Cut a tangled skein of jute with a sharp knife and it will be orderly and tidy. That's a good way to solve the difficult question."

When Gao Yang grew up, he became the emperor of Bei Qi state.

第六课

张良拾鞋

张良是秦汉时期①的人，是汉朝的开国功臣。

张良原是韩国人，韩国被秦所灭，张良一心想刺杀秦始皇为国报仇，结果没有成功，只好躲藏在乡下。

一天他正在一座桥上走，碰见一个白胡子老头坐在桥头。老头看见张良过来，把脚往桥头上一伸，他的一只鞋就掉到桥下去了。老头对张良说："喂，小伙子，下去把我的鞋捡上来。"张良听了很吃惊，心想：哪有这样不懂礼貌的人？可又一想：这位老人胡子都白了，就帮他一下吧。于是下桥把鞋子拾了起来。当张良恭恭敬敬地把鞋子给他时，老人把脚一伸，又说："帮我穿上。"张良真想发火，但还是忍住了，想：年轻人为老人干点活，有什么不好呢？于是就给他穿上了。老人笑笑，一句感谢的话都没说就走了。

---

① 秦汉时期——指秦朝（前221年—前206年）和汉朝（前206年—220年）的一段历史时期。

张良觉得奇怪，就一直跟在老头后面走。走了一里地，老头回身对张良说："你这个小伙子还不错，心地善良，又有耐心，我可以教导教导你。这样吧，过五天，天亮的时候，你再到桥上来见我。"张良知道碰上了有学问的人，连忙跪在老人面前，回答："是，先生。"

第五天，天刚亮张良就起床，赶到桥头，谁知老人已经等在那里了。他见张良这时候才来，生气地说："年轻人，跟老人约会，就该早点来，怎么倒叫我等你呢？"张良慌忙下跪认错。老人说："今天就算了，再过五天早一点来。"说完，头也不回就走了。

薛智广 画

又过了五天，张良没等天亮，就急急忙忙向桥头走去，谁知还没上桥，就看见老人又等在那里了。老人瞪了张良一眼，很不高兴地说："怎么回事？年轻人，又叫我等你这么久？"张良刚想道歉，老人说："不用说了，你再过五天再来。"

五天时间很快就过了四天，第四天夜里张良连觉都不敢睡，他在屋子里走来走去。刚过半夜，张良就赶到桥头。这一次，老人终于赶在老人前面了。张良在桥上等了一会儿，老人才来。他十分高兴地说："这样就对了。"老人说完，拿出一部书给张良说："这是一部非常珍贵的书，我送给你，你回去好好读，将来一定能成大事。我等着你的好消息。"

张良回去一看，原来是西周①姜太公②写的《太公兵法》。此后，张良用心读这部书，熟悉了用兵之道。几年后，张良帮助刘邦推翻了秦朝，建立了汉朝。

---

① 西周——中国历史上的一个朝代（约为公元前11世纪—前771年）。
② 姜太公——周朝初年的政治家，姓姜名尚(chū)，字子牙，俗(sú)称姜太公，是建立周朝的功臣。

中国古代故事

生词

gōng chén 功臣	hero	nài xīn 耐心	patience
hán 韩	Han State	jiào dǎo 教导	instruct
bào chóu 报仇	revenge	yuē huì 约会	make an appointment
jié guǒ 结果	as a result	dào qiàn 道歉	apologize
chī jīng 吃惊	be amazed	xiāo xi 消息	news
lǐ mào 礼貌	courtesy, politeness	jiāng 姜	*surname*
dǒng 懂	know, understand	shú xī 熟悉	know well, be familiar with
shí 拾	pick up	liú bāng 刘邦	Liu Bang, founder of the Western Han Dynasty
gōng jìng 恭敬	respectfully	tuī fān 推翻	overthrow
shàn liáng 善良	kind-hearted	jiàn lì 建立	found, establish

听写

功臣　报仇　拾鞋　懂　耐心　善良　约会　礼貌

吃惊　消息　*道歉　熟悉

比一比

报 { 报仇 / 报纸

功 { 用功 / 成功

敬 { 恭敬 / 尊敬

客 { 客气 / 客人

约 { 约会 / 大约

良 { 良好 / 善良

耐 { 忍耐 / 耐心

熟 { 熟悉 / 熟练

消 { 消息 / 消灭

字词运用

报纸

爸爸常常一边吃早饭一边看报纸。

我能读中文报纸，也能读英文报纸。

今天报纸的头条新闻是"神舟六号飞船上天"。

善良

马良有一颗善良的心，他常常帮穷人画鸡鸭、画牛羊。

爷爷是一位善良的老人，每天放学时他都在路边照看小朋友过马路。

 中国古代故事

词语解释

懂——知道，明白。

教导——教育、指导。

熟悉——知道得很清楚。

道歉——说对不起。

发火——因为生气而吵闹、骂人。

读一读，并记住

暖暖和和　大大方方　干干净净　许许多多

明明白白　说说笑笑　高高兴兴　舒舒服服(shū)

1. 窗外飘着鹅毛大雪，可屋子里暖暖和和的。

2. 小妹妹只有八岁，可是上台唱歌却大大方方。

3. 哥哥的作业总是写得干干净净。

4. 奶奶种了许许多多美丽的花。

5. 纸上明明白白写着两个大字"休息"。

6. 一路上大家说说笑笑，一点也不累。

7. 下课了，同学们在院子里高高兴兴地玩球。

8. 放假了，我要舒舒服服地睡上一大觉。

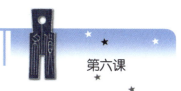

阅读

摸 钟

古时候，有一位很能干的县官。一天，有人告状，说家里被偷了。县官问明情况，很快抓来几个人，但他们都说自己没有偷。县官想来想去，想出了一个好办法。城外古庙里有一口大钟。当时的老百姓都相信这口大钟很神，能认出贼(zéi)。

县官把这几个人带到古庙，向大钟行了礼，然后说："现在，你们轮(lún)流去摸大钟。谁偷谁没偷，大钟一清二楚。没偷东西的，摸到大钟时它不出声；谁要是偷了东西，一摸它就会响。"说完，让他们一个一个走进屋里去摸钟。这几个人一个个摸完了钟，但是大钟一直没有出声音。

薛智广 画

大家以为没事，可以回去了。县官说："大家把手伸出来让我看看。"好多人的手都黑了，只有一个人的手是干净的。县官大喝一声："东西就是你偷的！"

那人吓了一跳，说："老爷，我没偷东西。"县官哈哈大笑说："大钟是铜(tóng)的，怎么会认贼呢！是我叫人在大钟上涂了黑。没偷东西的人，他们不怕大钟出声音，用手去摸，手就会黑。只有你偷了东西，不敢摸钟，你的两只手自然是干净的了。"

这个人听了，马上跪在地上认罪。

Lesson Six　Zhang Liang Picking up the Shoes

　　Zhang Liang, who lived in Qin and Han Dynasty, was a founding father of Han Dynasty.

　　Zhang Liang, originally a person from Han State, which has been invaded by Qin State, was determined to murder the Emperor Qin Shi Huang to revenge for his own country. But he failed and had to hide in the countryside.

　　One day, when he went across the bridge, a white-beard old man was sitting on the bridge. Seeing Zhang Liang coming over, he deliberately stretched his foot and one shoe fell down the bridge. The old shouted at him, "Hi, dear fellow, please go down and pick up my shoe." Greatly surprised, Zhang Liang thought by himself: How could this person be so impolite? On the other hand, he thought this man's beard had been white and just gave him a little help. So he went to pick the shoe up for the old man. But when he gave it to him with great respect, the old man stretched out his foot, "Help me put it on, please." Zhang Liang really got irritated, but he still kept his temper by thinking that it would be good for the young people to do something for the old. So he just helped him wear that shoe. With a laugh, the old man went away, without saying any words to show gratitude.

　　Feeling somewhat strange, Zhang Liang just followed the old man. Walking for about a mile, the old man turned his head and said, "You are a good lad, kind-hearted and patient. I decide to teach you something and come to see me on the bridge five days later". Knowing that he met a knowledgeable man, Zhang Liang knelt down in front of the old man to answer repeatedly, "Sure, sir."

　　On the fifth day, Zhang Liang immediately got up as soon as it dawned, but when he hurried to the bridge, the old man was already waiting for him there. Seeing Zhang Liang came so late, the old man got

angry and said, "Young man, you should be here earlier since you made an appointment with the old man. How could you keep me waiting ?" Zhang Liang pled for guilty on his knees. The old man said, "That's all right today. Come here a little earlier five days later." Without turning his head, the old man went away of his own.

Five days later, Zhang Liang hurried to the bridge before it dawned. Unexpectedly, the old man was already there waiting when he arrived. Staring at Zhang Liang, the old man was not very happy, "What's the matter, young man? How could you make me waiting for you for such a long time?" Before Zhang Liang had the time to apologize, the old man said, "You needn't explain and come here again five days later."

Four days passed and on the fourth night, Zhang Liang dared not go to sleep and just went to and forth in the room. He hurried to the bridge before it was just midnight. This time he came ahead of the old man. A moment later, the old man showed up and felt very happy, "This is good." Then he took out a book and gave it to Zhang Liang, "This is a valuable book and I give it to you. Go back and have a close reading of it, and you will be bound to be successful in future. I'll wait for your good news."

The book was *The Military Strategies of Tai Gong* written by Jiang Tai Gong, who is a famous politician and strategist in Western Zhou Dynasty. From that time on, Zhang Liang read into this book and mastered the art of employing military forces. Several years later, Zhang Liang helped Liu Bang to set up Han Dynasty by overthrowing Qin Dynasty.

Touching the Bell

In ancient times, there was an able county magistrate. One day, a person brought an action into the court, saying that his to house was robbed. After investigation, several people were caught, but they all denied that they didn't rob anything. After much thought, the magistrate thought out a good idea. It was said that there was a big bell in an old temple outside of the city, which was believed to tell a thief from the public.

Therefore, the magistrate took these people into the ancient temple, saluted to the big bell and said, "Now, listen, you all go to touch the bell in turns. The bell can tell who is the thief. The bell will not ring if those who haven't stolen anything touch it and the bell will immediately ring as soon as the thief touches it. " Then all of them went into the temple to touch the bell one by one. But the bell did not ring after all of them touched it and people thought they could go home.

At this moment, the magistrate said, "Let me have a look of your hands." Most people's hands got black and only one man's hands were clean. Seeing this, the magistrate shouted angrily at this man, "You are the thief!"

The man was surprised and denied, "Your Majesty, I didn't steal anything." Falling into a great laughter, the magistrate disclosed the truth, "Actually, the big bell is bronze and how can it tell the thief? I have the bell painted some ink. Not being afraid of the bell ringing, those who haven't stolen things will touch the bell and get hands black. Only you, dare not touch the bell and your hands are clean, because you stole the things."

Having nothing to explain, the man had to plead for guilty on his knees.

中国古代故事

第七课

三试华佗（huà tuó）

华佗是三国时期的名医。他发明了麻醉药。

华佗小时家里很穷，父亲很早就死了，华佗跟着母亲过活。一年，母亲得了怪病，医生也治不了，眼看着母亲痛苦地死去。从此，他立志学医救人。

华佗听说有位道人精通医术，名叫治华。他不怕山高路远，走了一个月，找到治华道人①。治华道人问他："学医很苦，你真的想学吗？"华佗说："我不怕苦，真心，诚心。"治华说："既然你真心，就先干几年杂活吧。"治华带他来到一个大院子，华佗一看，不由得大吃一惊：里面到处躺着病人，长疮流脓的，断腿出血的……什么病人都有。治华道人说："你要烧水，刷盆，照看病人。"华佗二话没说，就干了起来。不论刮风下雨，白天黑夜，他从不离开病人。师傅给病人吃什么药，他都一一记在心里。

---

① 道人——对道士的尊称。道士是道教的宗教（zōng zhí）职业者。

三年过去了，治华道人把华佗带到一个堆满药书、挂满图表的大房子，说："读书不能心急，你就在这里认真读书吧。"

冬去春来，三年又过去了。华佗读书从不偷懒。一天晚上，华佗正在看书，有人跑来说："师傅病重，你快去看看吧。"华佗赶去一看，师傅躺在床上。大家乱作一团，谁也不知道师傅得了什么病。华佗走到床头，摸了一下脉，笑着说："大家放心，师傅没病。"这时治华道人坐了起来，说："我的确没病，只是试试你们的。"大家非常佩服华佗。

正说话间，忽然书房里着火了。大家冲进去，七手八脚地拍灭了大火，可是已经晚了，许多藏书被烧成了灰。众师兄非常心疼。华佗想：幸好自己把医书全背熟了，现在可以重新默写出来。于是他开始默写医书。许多天过去了，他终于把烧掉的医书都默写出来了。

薛智广 画

当他把这件事告诉师傅时，治华道人笑着说："那火是我让人点的。不过烧掉的不是医书，只想考考你书读得怎样了。现在你通过了三次考试，真的学成了，我不再留你了。"

华佗告别了师傅，开始了治病救人的生涯。

生词

fā míng 发明	invent		duī mǎn 堆满	stack
má zuì yào 麻醉药	anaesthesia		tú biǎo 图表	chart
tòng kǔ 痛苦	pain		tōu lǎn 偷懒	be lazy, goldbrick
lì zhì 立志	aspire		dí què 的确	indeed
jīng tōng 精通	be proficient in		zhòng 众	many
yī shù 医术	art of healing, medical skills		xìng hǎo 幸好	fortunately
chéng xīn 诚心	wholeheartedness, sincere desire		mò xiě 默写	write from memory
zá huó 杂活	odd job		kǎo shì 考试	test
zhǎng chuāng 长疮	have a boil, affected by scabies		gào bié 告别	say goodbye to
liú nóng 流脓	suppurate		shēng yá 生涯	career, profession
shī fu 师傅	master			

听写

立志　医术　精通　诚心　杂活　的确　痛苦　考试
默写　众　告别　堆满　幸好　*麻醉药

比一比

偷 { 偷东西 / 偷懒 }　　脉 { 摸脉 / 山脉 }　　杂 { 复杂 / 杂活 }

刷 { 刷盆 / 刷子 }　　默 { 默写 / 沉默 }　　别 { 别人 / 告别 }

诚 { 诚实 / 诚心 }　　幸 { 幸好 / 幸福 }　　术 { 医术 / 算术 }

字词运用

救　求

1. 他跳入冰冷的水中去救人。
2. 奶奶虽然年岁大了，但是尽量自己做事，很少求人。

农　脓

1. 这里的农民用机器种地。
2. 她的伤口一直在流脓。

多音字

dí	de
的	的
的确	我的

词语解释

立志——树立志向。

精通——对一门学问、技术有深刻的了解和掌握。

杂活——各种各样不太重要的活。

读一读，并记住

清清楚楚　　平平安安　　端端正正

辛辛苦苦　　整整齐齐　　恭恭敬敬

1. 小平的作业总是写得整整齐齐、清清楚楚。

2. 哥哥总算平平安安地回来了。

3. 课堂上，同学们都坐得端端正正的，认真地听讲。

4. 华佗的父亲很早就死了，是母亲辛辛苦苦把他带大。

5. 小华特别爱干净，总是把自己的房间收拾得整整齐齐的。

6. 丽丽是一个懂礼貌的孩子，对老师总是恭恭敬敬的。

阅读

捉妖怪（yāo）

唐朝时候，有一个和尚，在屋里放了一个磬(qìng)。说来奇怪，这磬常常会自己响。那和尚以为是什么妖精在作怪，吓得生了病。

一天，一个姓曹的朋友来看望他。那和尚就一五一十地把磬的事对他说了。正说着，磬又响了起来。

曹先生不相信有什么妖(yāo)怪。他走过去把磬看了又看，听了又听。忽然，他拔腿就往大殿上跑。正好这个时候有人烧香，敲响了大殿上的那口大钟。说也奇怪：那大钟一响，和尚屋里的磬也跟着响；大钟不响了，屋里的磬也跟着不响了。他一下明白了，

薛智广 画

回到屋里对和尚说："我有办法除妖了。"他找来一把钢锉(cuò)，在磬上这儿锉几下，那儿锉几下，说："放心吧，以后这个磬再不会自己响了。"和尚不信，说："你别开玩笑了，你在磬上锉那么几下子，就能把妖怪捉到？"

曹先生说："这个磬自己会响，是因为它的'律(lǜ)'跟殿上那口大钟的'律'相同。所以殿上一敲钟，这个磬就会跟着响。现在，我用锉子锉了几下，磬和钟的律就不同了。以后再敲钟，磬就不会跟着响了。"果然，那个磬后来就再也不自己响了。和尚心里一块石头落了地，病也好了。

Lesson Seven　Three Trials on Hua Tuo

Hua Tuo, who had invented anaesthesia, was a well-known doctor in the period of Three Kingdoms. When Hua Tuo was a little boy, his father was dead and he lived a very poor life with his mother. One year, his mother caught a strange disease which couldn't be cured. Seeing his mother die very painfully, Hua Tuo was heart-broken and determined to be a doctor to save the people's life.

Having heard that there was a holy man named Zhi Hua who mastered consummate medical skills, Hua Tuo made up his mind to look for him despite of long distance. Walking for about one month, Hua Tuo found Zhi Hua at last and wanted to be his apprentice. Zhi Hua asked him, "It is an arduous task to be a doctor. Are you being serious?" "Yes, I fear no difficulties and hardships. I'm sincere and honest." Then Zhi Hua said, "Since you've made up your mind, then you just do some odd jobs for some years first." Leading Hua Tuo to a big yard, where patients were lying here and there, Zhi Hua told Hua Tuo, "You should boil water, wash the basins and take care of the patients." Greatly surprised to see so many patients who were blooding, growing boils and running with pus or leg-broken, Hua Tuo didn't say any-thing and began to work without complaint. He never left the patients whether in bad weather or at night and memorized every detail of how the master treated different patients.

Three years passed and Zhi Hua took Hua Tuo to a big house where is full of medical books and diagrams, said "You just stay here and read books patiently."

Winters went and springs came. Three years have passed and Hua Tuo read the books very assiduously. One night when he was reading, a person hurried to him, "Hurry up! The master was seriously ill." Hua Tuo immediately rushed to the master, who was already unconsciously lying in bed. All the people were in great confusion and didn't know what's the trouble with the master. Hua Tuo remained very calm, felt the master's pulse and said with a laugh, "You needn't worry and our master is all right." Hearing this, Zhi Hua sat up, said "Yes, I wasn't sick and just wanted to have a try on you." All the people admired Hua Tuo very much.

Just at this moment, the study was on fire. When people rushed there to put out the fire in a turmoil, it was too late and many medical book have been burned to ashes, which made all the learners there very sad. Hua Tuo thought to himself: Fortunately, I have recited all the medical books and should immediately write them from the memory. Many days passed and Hua Tuo managed to write all the books again.

When Hua Tuo told this event to the master, the master said with a laugh, "I have the fire lighted. I did not intend to burn the books, but to test how well you have studied them. Now I think you are skillful enough to leave me."

Feeling reluctant to say goodbye to the master, Hua Tuo began his career of saving people's life by curing their diseases.

Getting Rid of the Monster

In Tang Dynasty, there was a monk who put a qing (an ancient percussion instrument made of jade or stone, shaped like a carpenter's square) in the room. Strangely, the qing often rang of itself, which scared the monk to sickness. The monk thought it must be done by some monster.

One day, when a friend whose surname is Cao went to visit the monk, the monk told him everything about this case. Just at that moment, the qing was ringing again.

Mr. Cao, not believing there was some monster, went to have a good look of the qing and listened carefully to its sound. All of a sudden, he rushed towards the main hall of the temple, where he found the big bell was ringing and a person was burning incense and praying to Buddha. Strangely, when the bell rang, the qing in the monk's room rang as well; when the bell didn't make a sound, the qing remained silent too. Thinking for a short while, Mr. Cao got to know the truth. He rushed back to the monk's room and said, "I had an idea to get rid of the monster." With the words, he found a file and file the qing here and there, said "Just be assured that this qing will not ring of itself any more." Not convinced, the monk said, " Are you kidding? You just filed the qing in several places and could the monster be driven away?"

Mr. Cao explained the case, "This qing will ring of itself just because its rhythm goes at the same rate with that of the big bell in the main hall of the temple. So when the bell rings, the qing will ring as well. After I filed the qing, their rhythms became different. From now on, the qing will not ring with the bell." As expected, the qing have never rung of itself after that. The monk felt relieved and got recovered from the fear.

第八课

谁偷了茄子

明朝有个农民一大早去自己家的菜地干活。刚到菜地附近，他就看见一个青年挑着两筐茄子急匆匆地走了。他赶快跑到自己的菜地一看，地被踩得乱七八糟，茄子被摘走了好多，有好几棵茄子秧(yāng)连枝都被折断了。他追上那个青年，问："你怎么偷我的茄子？"那青年人说："这是我自己的茄子，这茄子上边写着你的名字吗？"

两个人拉拉扯扯就去找县官评理。

县官听他们各自把事情讲了一遍，然后让人把筐里的茄子都倒在地上，粗粗一看，就指着青年人说："这茄子分明是你偷的，还不承认！"人们都不明白老爷为什么这么说。那个青年也喊冤，说："老爷，这茄子确实是我自己种的呀！"县官冷笑一声说："这茄子真要是你种的，你会舍得把小茄子也摘下来去卖吗？你再看看，摘茄子的时候也不爱惜，连枝叶都劈下来了，可

薛智广 画

见这茄子不是你辛苦流汗种出来的。"那青年又说:"因为摘茄子的时候天黑,我看不清。"县官见那青年不承认,就生气地对他说:"你现在把这些茄子分成大中小三等,数一数各有多少个。如果数错了,重打四十大板!"青年人觉得这太容易了,就数起来。

这时,县官立刻派人和菜农一起去菜地里数刚摘掉的茄子把儿。结果,茄子把儿的数目和青年数的茄子数完全一样。那青年无话可说,只得承认了。

中国古代故事

生 词

qié zi 茄子	eggplant	fēn míng 分明	clearly
jí cōng cōng 急匆匆	hurriedly	chéng rèn 承认	admit
cǎi 踩	trample	hǎn yuān 喊冤	cry out one's grievances
luàn qī bā zāo 乱七八糟	in a mess	ài xī 爱惜	cherish
zhāi 摘	pick off	pǐ 劈	cleave
zhé duàn 折断	break off	róng yì 容易	easy
cū cū 粗粗	carelessly	bà r 把儿	petiole

听写

茄子　急匆匆　踩　乱七八糟　折断　容易　分明

拉扯　承认　爱惜　*摘

比一比

菜 { 种菜 / 白菜 / 饭菜 }　　　农 { 农民 / 农业 / cūn 农村 }　　　认 { 认真 / 认识 / 承认 }

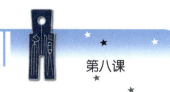

$$\begin{cases} 采（采花）\\ 彩（彩虹）\\ 踩（乱踩）\end{cases} \quad \begin{cases} 枝（树枝）\\ 支（一支）\\ 技（技术）\end{cases} \quad \begin{cases} 平（平常）\\ 苹（苹果）\\ 评（评理）\end{cases}$$

词语解释

急匆匆——急忙。

乱七八糟——非常乱。

辛苦——工作多、时间长，身心劳累。

爱惜——觉得珍贵，舍不得多用或破坏。

思考题

县官用什么办法来证明那个青年人真的偷了茄(zhèng)子？

标点符号介绍

1. 句号（。）表示一个陈述(shù)句完(liǎo)了。
2. 逗(dòu)号（，）表示句子中的停顿。
3. 冒号（：）用以提示下文。
4. 引号（""）表示直接引用的部分。
5. 惊叹号（！）表示强烈的感情或一个感叹句完了。

 中国古代故事

读一读，注意标点符号

　　小青蛙跟着妈妈游到桥底下，看到周围美丽的景色，高兴得叫起来："呱呱呱，多好啊！"这时，不知哪儿有一只小青蛙也在叫："呱呱呱，多好啊！"小青蛙问："你是谁？你在哪儿？"那只看不见的小青蛙也在问："你是谁？你在哪儿？"妈妈对小青蛙说："傻孩子，那是你的回声。"

组字并拼音

1. 三个"人"组成众，读（ zhòng ）
2. 三个"口"组成品，读（　　　）
3. 三个"日"组成晶，读（　　　）
4. 三个"石"组成磊，读（　　　）
5. 三个"木"组成森，读（　　　）

李子是苦的

王戎(róng)是中国古代有名的文人。

王戎7岁的时候和几个小朋友出去玩。玩了半天，大家又累又渴。突然，有人看见大路边有一棵李子树，树上结满了李子。大家飞快地向李子树跑去，只有王戎没有去。

大家跑到树下就摘李子。这时，王戎走过来，小朋友们把李子给他，他不吃，说："这李子是苦的，不能吃。"大家谁也不信。有个小朋友急忙咬了一口，可是马上又吐(tǔ)了出来，生气地说："苦的！"

大家非常奇怪，问王戎："你怎么知道李子是苦的？难道你吃过？"王戎说："没吃过。但是我想，路边上的李子树长的李子如果是甜的，早就被过路的人摘完了。"大家听了以后都觉得很有道理。

中国古代故事

English Translation

Lesson Eight   Who Stole the Eggplants?

In Ming Dynasty, there was a farmer who went to his vegetable plot one morning. When he was near the plot, he saw a young man leaving in a hurry by carrying two baskets of eggplants. He immediately rushed to his own plot and found the plot was trodden terribly. Most of his eggplants had been picked up and some of the branches had been broken. Then he ran after that young man and questioned him, "How could you steal my eggplants?" "These are my own eggplants. How could you say they are yours? Can you find your name on the eggplants?"Argued the young man.

They fell into quarrel with each other and went to the local court for fair judgment.

The officer of the county listened to their report and then had the eggplants of baskets emptied onto the ground. Having a rough look of eggplants, the officer pointed at the young man, shouting "It is obvious that you stole the eggplants. Why not hurry to admit it?" People got confused and the young man also cried out about the unfair judgment, "Your Majesty, the eggplants are really planted by myself!" The officer said with a cold laugh, " If the eggplants are really your own, do you grudge picking up the small ones? Besides, the branch and leaves are picked up, which shows that you do not cherish them because they are not the eggplants you grow with sweat by yourself. " The young man contended, "Since it is dark, I couldn't see it clearly." Seeing the young man not admitting the guilt, the officer got very angry and said, "Now you sort them out in three categories: big, middle and small. Count them respectively and tell me the number of eggplants in each category. If you make any mistake, you'll be spanked 40 times." The young man thought that was an easy task and began to count.

At the same time, the officer sent the farmer and other officer to count the petioles of the eggplants in the vegetable plot. It turned out the two figures are totally equal. Facing the fact, the young man had nothing to argue any more and had to admit the guilt.

The Plum Is Bitter

Wang Rong was a well-known man of letters in ancient China.

When he was seven years old, he went out to play with several friends. After playing for some time, they felt tired and thirsty. All of a sudden, a kid saw a plum tree beside the road which grows many plums, so all the kids ran towards the plum tree except Wang Rong.

All the kids were busy picking up the plums when Wang Rong came under the tree. One kid gave him a plum, but Wang Rong didn't accept it and said, "It is bitter and you can't eat." Nobody believed that. One kid just hurried to bite it and immediately spit it out, shouting angrily, "It is too bitter!"

Feeling very surprised, all the kids asked Wang Rong, "How could you know the plum is bitter? Have you ever tasted it?" "No," answered Wang Rong, "But I guess, if the plums are sweet, they must have been already picked up since the tree is just beside the road." All the kids were convinced and felt such analysis made sense.

第九课

七步诗

曹丕(pī)和曹植都是曹操的儿子。

曹植很聪明，诗歌文章写得又多又好。大家都很佩服曹植，称他是文学家。曹操也很喜爱他，只有曹丕忌妒他。

曹操死后，曹丕做了皇帝。有一天曹植来见哥哥。曹丕没好气地说："我和你虽然是亲兄弟，但是从礼节上来说，是君臣。以后可不许你仗着自己的才学，不讲君臣的礼节啊！"

薛智广 画

中国古代故事

曹植低着头,小心地回答:"是"。曹丕又说:"父亲在世的时候,你常常拿诗歌文章在别人面前夸耀。我问你,那些诗文是不是请别人写的?"曹植说:"我从来没有请人帮忙,都是自己写的。"

曹丕板着脸说:"好!现在我叫你作一首诗。你走七步,七步走完了,就必须把诗作出来。要不然就治你的罪。"曹植知道曹丕想害他,说:"请出个题目"。曹丕没想到他答应得这么快,心想:好,我就出个难的,看你怎样作!他对曹植说:"我和你是兄弟,就用'兄弟'做题目。可是,诗里面不许带有'兄弟'这两个字。"

曹植回答了一声"是!"就走起步来。走一步,念一句,七步还没走完,诗就作出来了:

煮豆燃豆萁(qí),

豆在釜中泣:

本是同根生,

相煎何太急?

这首诗的意思是:

煮豆子烧的是豆秸(jiē)呀,

豆子在锅里伤心地哭泣:

我们本是同一个根上长出来的啊，

你为什么这样着急煮我？

在这首诗里，曹植把曹丕比做豆秸，把自己比做豆子，等于说：我们本来是亲兄弟啊，你为什么要这样害我呢？

曹丕听完曹植的诗，脸红了，虽然心里不高兴，但是他不能治曹植的罪。

生词

wénzhāng 文章	article	tímù 题目	topic; subject
jìdù 忌妒	envy	bìxū 必须	must; have to
lǐjié 礼节	etiquette	rán 燃	burn
zhàngzhe 仗着	depend on	fǔ 釜	pot
kuāyào 夸耀	ostentate	jiān 煎	simmer in water
bǎnzheliǎn 板着脸	keep a straight face	dòujiē 豆秸	beanstalk
zhìzuì 治罪	punish sb. for his crime	kūqì 哭泣	cry

听写

文章　板着脸　治罪　题目　燃　哭泣　必须

礼节　*妒

中国古代故事

比一比

文 { 文章, 文化, 中文 }

伤 { 伤心, 悲伤, 受伤 }

题 { 题目, 问题, 数学题 }

痛 { 痛苦, 痛快 }

礼 { 礼貌, 礼服 }

节 { 礼节, 节日 }

字词运用

结果

妈妈让妹妹少吃糖,她不听,结果牙坏了。

容易

白色的衣服容易脏。

做事情马虎就容易出错。

必须

医生对病人说:"你必须按时吃药。"

上飞机前必须经过安全检(chá)查。

妈妈对小春说:"十点以前你必须回家。"

词语解释

忌妒—— 因为别人比自己好而恨(hèn)别人。

治罪——定罪名并处罚。

标点符号介绍

1. 问号（？）用在疑问句之后。
2. 顿号（、）表示句中并列的词或词组之间的停顿。
3. 分号（；）表示句中并列分句之间的停顿。
4. 省略(lüè)号（……）表示文中省略的部分。

读一读，注意标点符号

1. 小燕子惊奇地叫起来："小山雀，你怎么吃树皮呀？"
2. 这座山上有松树、杨树、苹果树、竹子等许多植物。
3. 访问上等的国家，就派上等的人去；访问下等的国家，就派下等人。
4. 中国有汉族、回族、蒙古族、藏族……共56个民族。

Lesson Nine The Seven-Step Poem

Cao Pi and Cao Zhi were two sons of Cao Cao.

Cao Zhi was gifted and very good at writing, so people all admired him and called him a man of letters. Cao Cao also liked him very much, which made his brother Cao Pi envy him.

After Cao Cao died, Cao Pi became the emperor. One day, his younger brother Cao Pi came to see him. But Cao Pi met him very impolitely, "We are brothers, but actually the relationship is between the monarch and the minister. From now on you are not allowed to show off your talent and should follow some etiquettes. "

Lowering his head, Cao Pi answered very timidly, "Yes." Then Cao Pi continued, "When father was alive, you often showed off in public by your good poems. Now I ask you, did you ask the others to write those for you?" "No, " said Cao Zhi, "I never asked for the other's help and I did it all by myself."

Pulling a long face, Cao Pi said, "All right. Now I order you to make a poem within the time limit of taking seven steps. Otherwise, you'll be severely punished. " Scenting his brother's intension of getting rid of him, Cao Pi said, "Please give me a topic." Not expecting him to agree in such a short time, Cao Pi thought: That's good. I'll give you a difficult topic and see how you can make it. So he said, "You and I are brothers, so you just take "brothers" as the title. But the word "brother" should not be included in the lines of poem. "

"All right!" with the words, Cao Zhi began to move in the room. Taking one step, he read aloud one line. Before he finished seven steps, he made the poem like this:

煮豆燃豆萁，

豆在釜中泣：

本是同根生，

相煎何太急？

It means: People burn beanstalks to boil beans,

The beans in the pot cry out sadly.

Born as we are of the same root,

Why should you torment me so fiercely?

In this poem, Cao Zhi compared Cao Pi to the beanstalk and himself to the bean. In other words, we are actually brothers, why should you torture me like this?

Hearing this poem, Cao Pi got shamefully flushed and couldn't punish Cao Zhi as he originally intended.

生字表(简)

1. 冲 官 员 议 杆 秤 或 者 宰 切 艘 舷
2. 忌 输 垂 丧 败 锣 赢 序
3. 寄 杀 毒 巫 胆 除 剑 斗 举 砍 溅 勇 编
4. 侮 辱 显 示 矮 访 袖 既 规 矩 犯 罪 盗 柑 取 尊
5. 魏 豹 荒 娶 淹 绅 硬 扮 席 泪 催 跪 饶 渠 浇
6. 韩 仇 惊 貌 懂 拾 恭 敬 善 耐 歉 消 息
7. 姜 悉 邦 推
8. 醉 痛 志 医 诚 疮 脓 傅 堆 试 众 幸 默 考 涯
9. 茄 匆 踩 摘 折 承 冤 惜 劈
10. 章 妒 耀 必 须 燃 釜 煎 秸 泣

共计114个生字

生字表（繁）

1. 沖(chōng) 官(guān) 員(yuán) 議(yì) 桿(gǎn) 秤(chèng) 宰(zǎi) 或(huò) 者(zhě) 切(qiē) 艘(sōu) 舷(xián)

2. 忌(jì) 輸(shū) 垂(chuí) 喪(sàng) 敗(bài) 鑼(luó) 贏(yíng) 序(xù)

3. 寄(jì) 殺(shā) 毒(dú) 巫(wū) 膽(dǎn) 除(chú) 劍(jiàn) 鬥(dòu) 舉(jǔ) 砍(kǎn) 濺(jiàn) 勇(yǒng) 編(biān)

4. 侮(wǔ) 辱(rǔ) 顯(xiǎn) 示(shì) 矮(ǎi) 訪(fǎng) 袖(xiù) 既(jì) 規(guī) 矩(jǔ) 犯(fàn) 罪(zuì) 盜(dào) 柑(gān) 取(qǔ) 尊(zūn)

5. 魏(wèi) 豹(bào) 荒(huāng) 娶(qǔ) 淹(yān) 紳(shēn) 硬(yìng) 扮(bàn) 席(xí) 淚(lèi) 催(cuī) 跪(guì) 饒(ráo) 渠(qú) 澆(jiāo)

6. 韓(hán) 仇(chóu) 驚(jīng) 貌(mào) 懂(dǒng) 拾(shí) 恭(gōng) 敬(jìng) 善(shàn) 耐(nài) 歉(qiàn) 消(xiāo) 息(xī) 姜(jiāng) 悉(xī) 邦(bāng) 推(tuī)

7. 醉(zuì) 痛(tòng) 志(zhì) 醫(yī) 誠(chéng) 瘡(chuāng) 膿(nóng) 傅(fù) 堆(duī) 試(shì) 眾(zhòng) 幸(xìng) 默(mò) 考(kǎo) 涯(yá)

8. 茄(qié) 匆(cōng) 踩(cǎi) 摘(zhāi) 折(zhé) 承(chéng) 冤(yuān) 惜(xī) 劈(pǐ)

9. 章(zhāng) 妒(dù) 耀(yào) 必(bì) 須(xū) 燃(rán) 釜(fǔ) 煎(jiān) 秸(jiē) 泣(qì)

共計114個生字

生词表（简）

1. 曹冲 称一称 官员 到底 议论 杆秤 或者 宰切
   难道 连忙 赶 一艘 沿着 船舷 果然

2. 田忌 大将 各自 等级 输 垂头丧气 失败 锣
   第一场 赢 调换 顺序 转败为胜

3. 寄 杀 毒 官府 巫婆 胆大 除害 剑 咬 斗 举 砍
   鲜血 溅 勇敢 编

4. 出使 借机 侮辱 显示 威风 矮小 访问 迎接
   袖子 既然 规矩 犯人 犯罪 强盗 柑子 安居乐业
   取笑 尊重

5. 豹 魏国 管理 荒 娶亲 淹 官绅 硬 新娘
   打扮 草席 泪水 催 跪下 求饶 水渠 浇田

6. 功臣 韩国 报仇 结果 吃惊 礼貌 懂 拾 恭敬
   善良 耐心 教导 约会 道歉 消息 熟悉 刘邦 推翻
   建立

7.
| fā míng | má zuì yào | tòng kǔ | lì zhì | jīng tōng | yī shù | chéng xīn | zá huó |
| 发明 | 麻醉药 | 痛苦 | 立志 | 精通 | 医术 | 诚心 | 杂活 |

| zhǎng chuāng | liú nóng | shī fu | duī mǎn | tú biǎo | tōu lǎn | dí què | zhòng |
| 长疮 | 流脓 | 师傅 | 堆满 | 图表 | 偷懒 | 的确 | 众 |

| xìng hǎo | mò xiě | kǎo shì | gào bié | shēng yá |
| 幸好 | 默写 | 考试 | 告别 | 生涯 |

8.
| qié zi | jí cōngcōng | cǎi | luàn qī bā zāo | zhāi | zhé duàn | cū cū | fēn míng |
| 茄子 | 急匆匆 | 踩 | 乱七八糟 | 摘 | 折断 | 粗粗 | 分明 |

| chéng rèn | hǎn yuān | ài xī | pǐ | róng yì | bàr |
| 承认 | 喊冤 | 爱惜 | 劈 | 容易 | 把儿 |

9.
| wén zhāng | jì du | lǐ jié | zhàng zhe | kuā yào | bǎn zhe liǎn | zhì zuì | tí mù |
| 文章 | 忌妒 | 礼节 | 仗着 | 夸耀 | 板着脸 | 治罪 | 题目 |

| bì xū | rán | fǔ | jiān | dòu jiē | qì |
| 必须 | 燃 | 釜 | 煎 | 豆秸 | 泣 |

共计149个生词

生词表（繁）

1. 曹沖 稱一稱 官員 到底 議論 桿秤 或者 宰切
   難道 連忙 趕 一艘 沿著 船舷 果然

2. 田忌 大將 各自 等級 輸 垂頭喪氣 失敗 鑼
   第一場 贏 調換 順序 轉敗為勝

3. 寄 殺 毒 官府 巫婆 膽大 除害 劍 咬 鬥 舉 砍
   鮮血 濺 勇敢 編

4. 出使 借機 侮辱 顯示 威風 矮小 訪問 迎接
   袖子 既然 規矩 犯人 犯罪 強盜 柑子 安居樂業
   取笑 尊重

5. 豹 魏國 管理 荒 娶親 淹 官紳 硬 新娘
   打扮 草席 淚水 催 跪下 求饒 水渠 澆田

6. 功臣 韓國 報仇 結果 吃驚 禮貌 懂 拾 恭敬
   善良 耐心 教導 約會 道歉 消息 熟悉 劉邦 推翻
   建立

7. 發明(fā míng) 麻醉藥(má zuì yào) 痛苦(tòng kǔ) 立志(lì zhì) 精通(jīng tōng) 醫術(yī shù) 誠心(chéng xīn) 雜活(zá huó)

長瘡(zhǎng chuāng) 流膿(liú nóng) 師傅(shī fu) 堆滿(duī mǎn) 圖表(tú biǎo) 偷懶(tōu lǎn) 的確(dí què) 眾(zhòng)

幸好(xìng hǎo) 考試(kǎo shì) 默寫(mò xiě) 告別(gào bié) 生涯(shēng yá)

8. 茄子(qié zi) 急匆匆(jí cōngcōng) 踩(cǎi) 亂七八糟(luàn qī bā zāo) 摘(zhāi) 折斷(zhé duàn) 粗粗(cū cū) 分明(fēn míng)

承認(chéng rèn) 喊冤(hǎn yuān) 愛惜(ài xī) 劈(pǐ) 容易(róng yì) 把兒(bàr)

9. 文章(wén zhāng) 忌妒(jì dù) 禮節(lǐ jié) 仗著(zhàng zhe) 誇耀(kuā yào) 板著臉(bǎn zhe liǎn) 治罪(zhì zuì) 題目(tí mù)

必須(bì xū) 燃(rán) 釜(fǔ) 煎(jiān) 豆秸(dòu jiē) 泣(qì)

共計149個生詞

第一课

一 写生词

冲											
官	员										
议	论										
杆											
秤											
或	者										
宰											
切											
艘											
船	舷										

二 组词

期_____　　官_____　　沿_____　　称_____

秤_____　　冲_____　　或_____　　照_____

果_____　　切_____　　忙_____　　议_____

三 抄写课文(包括标点符号)

大象又高又大,身体像一面墙,腿像四根大粗柱子。这象到底有多重呢?官员们议论着。曹操问:"谁能有办法把这头大象称一称?"

四 选字组词

(称 秤)为　　一杆(称 秤)　　官(园 员)

花(园 圆)　　(主 柱)人　　石(主 柱)

主(腰 要)　　(提 捉)得起　　难(到 道)

五 选择填空（把词语写在空白处）

1. 上学别忘了_____着作业。（代　带　袋　戴）

2. 这件衣服上有个口_____。（代　带　袋）

3. 爷爷、爸爸和我是三_____人。（代　带　袋）

4. 外面刮着大风,你出去一定要_____帽子。

（代　带　戴）

5. 我每天都要站在_____上,_____体重。

（称一称　秤）

六 根据课文判断对错

1. 三国时期,有个著名的政治家叫曹操。　　___对___错

2. 曹操是曹冲的儿子。　　___对___错

3. 砍一棵树造杆大秤称象的主意很不错。　　___对___错

4. 把大象宰了切成块再称的主意不好。　　___对___错

5. 曹冲只有六岁,但是很聪明。　　___对___错

七 造句

1. 果然＿＿＿＿＿＿＿＿＿＿＿＿＿＿＿＿

2. 难道＿＿＿＿＿＿＿＿＿＿＿＿＿＿＿＿

3. 假如＿＿＿＿＿＿＿＿＿＿＿＿＿＿＿＿

八 根据阅读课文选择填空（把词语写在空白处）

1. 曹冲是曹操的＿＿＿＿＿＿。（孙子　儿子　女儿）

2. 曹操的马鞍子给＿＿＿＿＿＿咬破了。（虫子　老鼠）

3. 曹冲说："你别怕，我有办法＿＿＿＿＿＿你。"（救　求）

4. 曹冲用小刀在自己的＿＿＿＿＿＿上挖了几个小洞。（裤子　衣服）

5. 曹冲说："别人都说，穿老鼠＿＿＿＿＿＿破的衣服，人要生大病。"（狡　咬　校）

6. 曹操笑着说："那是＿＿＿＿＿＿人的，别信它。"（遍　骗）

7. 曹操说："老鼠嘛，还管得住它＿＿＿＿＿＿东西。"
（狡　咬　校）

九 缩写《曹冲称象》(最少五句)

十 朗读课文三遍

第三课

一 写生词

寄											
杀											
毒											
巫婆											
胆大											
除害											
剑											
咬											
斗											
举											
砍											
溅											

勇	敢										
编											

二 组词

毒_____　　府_____　　寄_____　　胆_____

剑_____　　凶_____　　除_____　　举_____

步_____　　咬_____　　血_____　　勇_____

斗_____　　编_____　　砍_____

三 抄写课文（包括标点符号）

聪明勇敢的李寄杀死了毒蛇，为民除害。老百姓感谢她，把她的故事编成歌，一直传唱着。

四 选字组词

(交 校)换　　(交 校)朋友　　学(交 校)

(咬 狡)人　　(咬 狡)猾　　(传 转)唱

五 先组字,再组词

"才"进口是(　)_____　　"大"进口是(　)_____

"冬"进口是(　)_____　　"元"进口是(　)_____

"玉"进口是(　)_____

六 选择填空(把词语写在空白处)

1. 大蛇_____出来伤人。

　A 常常　　B 长长

2. 小女孩叫_____,胆大过人。

　A 李奇　　B 李骑　　C 李寄　　D 季寄

3. 她_____米团、剑和猎犬去杀蛇。

　A 代　　B 带着　　C 戴着

4. 蛇吃米团时,李寄放出_____咬蛇。

　A 黑猪　　B 猎狗　　C 花猫

七 造句

   1. 勇敢＿＿＿＿＿＿＿＿＿＿＿＿＿＿＿＿＿＿＿＿

   2. 举起＿＿＿＿＿＿＿＿＿＿＿＿＿＿＿＿＿＿＿＿

八 根据阅读课文判断对错

1. 在中国南方的农村,你可以看到方块的水稻田。　　　＿＿对＿＿错

2. "田"字的写法,很像我们看到的水稻田。　　　＿＿对＿＿错

3. "男"字,是由"田"和"力"组成的。　　　＿＿对＿＿错

4. 古代中国是个农业国家,很多女人在田地里劳动。　　　＿＿对＿＿错

5. "子"字,在甲骨文中,是孩子小时候的样子:大大的头和一个小身子。　　　＿＿对＿＿错

6. "女"和"子"组成"好"字。　　　＿＿对＿＿错

九 缩写《李寄杀蛇》（最少五句）

十 做手工

十一 朗读课文三遍

第五课

一 写生词

魏											
豹											
荒											
娶	亲										
淹											
官	绅										
硬											
打	扮										
草	席										
泪	水										
催											
跪	下										

求	饶											
水	渠											
浇	田											

二 组词

管_____　　娶_____　　淹_____　　外_____

喜_____　　选_____　　扮_____　　领_____

新_____　　跪_____　　席_____　　渠_____

浇_____　　饶_____　　催_____　　泪_____

三 抄写课文，并听写（包括标点符号）

"有女儿的人家都逃到外地去了。这里的人口越来越少，地方也越来越穷。"西门豹想了想说："下一回河神娶亲，告诉我一声，我也去送送新娘。"

四 选字组词

（亲 新）爱　　（亲 新）房子　　（选 先）后

（取 娶）亲　　（荒 慌）地　　挑（选 先）

五 选择填空（把词语写在空白处）

1. 西门豹带领老百姓开水渠，引水_____田。（浇 饶）

2. 官绅们一个个吓得面如土色，跪下求_____。

（浇 饶）

3. 这本书老师让他读了三_____。（遍 骗）

4. 不能_____人。（遍 骗）

5. 今天的晚会，姑娘们打_____得十分漂亮。（扮 绊）

6. 上课时，老师_____了一个新同学。（领来 领土）

六 写出反义词

硬——　　　　　　本地——

高——　　　　　　胆大——

七 造句

不论……都……＿＿＿＿＿＿＿＿＿＿＿＿＿

＿＿＿＿＿＿＿＿＿＿＿＿＿＿＿＿＿＿＿＿＿

要是……就……＿＿＿＿＿＿＿＿＿＿＿＿＿

＿＿＿＿＿＿＿＿＿＿＿＿＿＿＿＿＿＿＿＿＿

八 词语解释

喜事——

九 根据课文判断对错

1. 西门豹是战国时期的人。　　　　　＿＿对＿＿错

2. 西门豹一看，女孩满脸泪水。　　　＿＿对＿＿错

3. 巫婆和官绅都是骗钱害人的。　　　＿＿对＿＿错

4. 河神娶亲的日子，西门豹救了那个新娘。　　　　　　　　　　　　　　＿＿对＿＿错

5. 西门豹真是个聪明的好官。　　　　＿＿对＿＿错

十　根据阅读课文判断对错

1. 一天，高欢给他的儿子一团乱麻，让他整理。　　　　　___对___错

2. 几个儿子拿着乱麻，理了老半天，谁也理不清。　　　　___对___错

3. 他的三儿子高洋向父亲要一把剑。　　___对___错

4. 高洋接过剑，向乱麻一剑砍下去。　　___对___错

5. 高洋说："要想把一团乱麻理清，完全是浪费工夫。"　　　　　　　　___对___错

十一　缩写课文《西门豹的故事》（最少五句）

_____
_____
_____
_____
_____
_____

十二 朗读课文三遍

第七课

一 写生词

麻	醉	药									
痛	苦										
立	志										
医	术										
诚	心										
长	疮										
流	脓										
师	傅										
堆	满										
众											
幸	好										
默	写										

考	试										
生	涯										

二 抄写课文(包括标点符号)

华佗想：幸好自己把医书全背熟了，现在可以重新默写出来。于是他开始默写医书。许多天过去了，他终于把烧掉的医书都默写出来了。

三 选字组词

麻(酒　醉)　　(辛　幸)好　　(默　黑)写

山(脉　永)　　(辛　幸)苦　　(默　黑)天

四 选择填空(把词语写在空白处)

1. 他跳入水中去_____人。(救　求)

2. 她一碰到困难就想_____。（求人　救人）

3. 我爸爸是农民,爷爷也是_____。（工人　农民）

4. 她的伤口已经好了,不再_____了。（流脓　流水）

5. 昆仑山是中国的一条大山_____。（脉　永）

五　词语解释

　　立志_____

　　精通_____

六　读一读下面的句子,写写你的看法

　　治华说:"读书不能心急,你就在这里认真读书吧。"

_____

_____

七　根据课文判断对错

1. 华佗是三国时期的名医。他发明了麻醉药。　　____对____错

2. 华佗母亲很早就死了。华佗跟着父亲过活。　　____对____错

3. 华佗的老师叫治华。　　____对____错

4. 华佗不愿意干杂活照看病人。　　____对____错

5. 老师让华佗快快读书。　　　　　　　　　　____对____错

6. 华佗可以默写医书。　　　　　　　　　　　____对____错

7. 眼看着母亲痛苦地死去,华佗立志学医救人。　　　　　　　　　　　　　　　　____对____错

8. 不论刮风下雨,白天黑夜,华佗从不离开病人。　　　　　　　　　　　　　　　　____对____错

八　根据阅读课文判断对错

1. 唐朝时候,有一个和尚,他的屋里有一个自己会响的磬。　　　　　　　　　　　　　____对____错

2. 因为磬自己会响,把和尚给吓哭了。　____对____错

3. 和尚的一个姓张的朋友到庙里看望和尚。　　　　　　　　　　　　　　　　____对____错

4. 曹先生不相信有什么妖(yāo)怪。　　____对____错

5. 曹先生用钢锉(cuò),在磬上锉了几下,磬就不再自己响了。　　　　　　　　　　____对____错

6. 和尚心里一块石头落了地,病也好了。　____对____错

7. 曹先生懂科学。　　　　　　　　　　____对____错

九　朗读课文三遍

第九课

一 写生词

文	章										
忌	妒										
夸	耀										
必	须										
燃											
釜											
煎											
豆	秸										
哭	泣										

二 组词

章_____ 佩_____ 妒_____ 仗_____

罪_____ 题_____ 夸_____ 礼_____

渠_____ 泣_____ 煎_____ 必_____

三 抄写课文(包括标点符号)

煮豆燃豆萁,豆在釜中泣:

本是同根生,相煎何太急?

四 选择填空(把词语写在空白处)

1. 这次考试,不但考语法,还考写_____。

(文学 文章 文化)

2. 中国_____已有五千年的历史了。

(文学 文章 文化)

3. 这次数学考试没有_____,都很容易。

(题目 难题)

4. 小弟弟_____奶奶喜欢他，就乱闹。（仗着　打仗）

5. 小学生应该讲卫生、守秩序并且有_____zhì_____。

（礼节　礼貌　礼服）

五　词语解释

忌妒_____

六　根据课文判断对错

1. 曹丕是曹植的哥哥。　　　　　　　　　___对___错

2. 曹丕忌妒曹植，因为曹植诗歌文章写得好。

___对___错

3. 曹丕做了皇帝，让曹植走七步，就作出一首

诗来。　　　　　　　　　　　　　　___对___错

4. 曹植七步还没走完，诗就作出来了。　　___对___错

5. 曹丕想害曹植，但是没有害成。　　　　___对___错

七　造句

文章_____

必须_____

八 给下面的两段文字点上标点

　　1. 蓝蓝的天空飘着一片片白云　山谷里有一条小河　河水慢慢地流着　不远的地方有一片绿色的竹林　竹林边开着一朵朵火红的野花　这里的空气多么新鲜　这里的风景多么美丽　这是什么地方　这是我可爱的家乡

　　2. 老黄雀把小虫喂到小黄雀的嘴里　那只小黄雀吃得可香了　它问妈妈　这是什么呀　真好吃　老黄雀说　这是卷(juǎn)叶虫　这种害虫很狡猾　它吐出丝　把树叶卷起来　自己躲在里面吃叶肉

九 缩写课文《七步诗》(最少五句)

_____
_____
_____
_____
_____

十 朗读课文三遍并背颂(sòng)《七步诗》

第一课听写

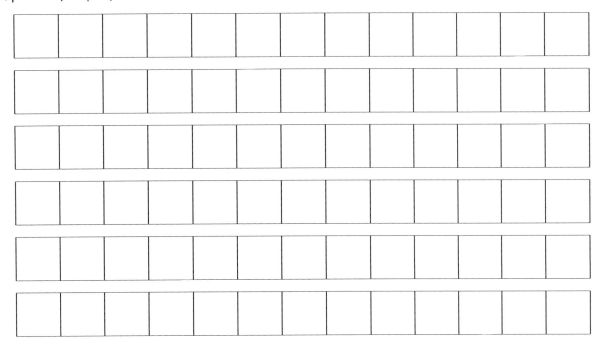

第三课听写

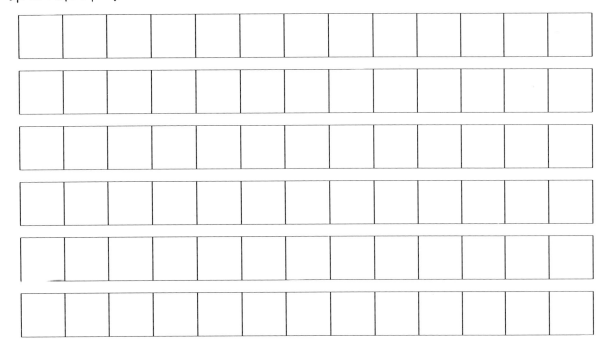

第五课听写

中国古代故事

第七课听写

第九课听写

练习纸

中国古代故事

《双双中文教材》是一套专门为海外学生编写的中文教材。它是由美国加州王双双老师和中国专家学者共同努力,在海外多年的实践中编写出来的。全书共20册,识字量2500个,包括了从识字、拼音、句型、短文的学习,到初步的较系统的中国文化的学习。教材大体介绍了中国地理、历史、哲学等方面的丰富内容,突出了中国文化的魅力。课本知识面广,趣味性强,深入浅出,易教易学。全套书均有CD-ROM。

这套教材体系完整、构架灵活、使用面广。学生可以从零起点开始,一直学完全部课程20册;也可以将后11册(10~20册)的九个文化专题和第五册(汉语拼音)单独使用,这样便于高中和大学开设中国哲学、地理、历史等专门课程以及假期班、短期中国文化班、拼音速成班使用。

本教材符合了美国AP中文课程的目标和基本要求。

这本《中国古代故事》是《双双中文教材》的第十二册,课本适用于已学习掌握800多个汉字的学生。全书共九课,教程为12~16学时(每学时1.5~2小时)。

本书介绍了15个中国古代故事。故事情节曲折,带有传奇色彩,反映了古代中国人的生活习俗和风貌,以及他们的聪慧和幽默。学生们通过学习,进一步提高了中文水平,也感受到古代先贤的心胸和智慧,开阔了思维,得到了文化的传承。

本书介绍了常用连词、形容词的重叠,以及汉语中最常用的几种标点符号,同时又增加了组字练习。两段趣味汉字短文介绍了汉字由来及演变。

ISBN 978-7-301-08712-1

全套定价:76.00元
(含课本、练习册和一张CD-ROM)